Phonetic Story 5

Short ŭ Words

Raceway Step 14

MODERN CURRICULUM PRESS

Pearson Learning Group

Contents

Gus the Bug

By Sue Dickson

Illustrated by Russell Benfanti

Vocabulary Words

1. bug
2. bun
3. bus
4. cup
5. cups
6. cut
7. drum
8. dug
9. dull
10. fun
11. Gus
12. have
13. hum

14. hut
15. mud
16. nut
17. of
18. puff
19. run
20. truck

Story Words

21. glass
21. milk
22. sip
23. sit
24. step

Gus is a bug.

Gus and his mom and his dad have a hut.
It is a nut.

Gus has a truck and
a bus.
Gus has fun in the truck.

Gus has a drum.
Gus can hum.
Mom said, "It is not dull
in the hut."

Gus has ham on a bun.
It is a big bun.
Mom will cut the bun.

Gus has milk.
Gus will sip his milk
in a glass.

Gus has fun.
Gus can run fast.

Gus will run to the hut.
Gus will puff a bit.

Gus will sit on the step to rest.

Next, Gus has fun
in the mud.
Gus dug and dug.

Gus dug six cups of mud!
Gus had a lot of fun
in the mud!

The End

Gus and Judd

By Sue Dickson
Illustrated by Russell Benfanti

Vocabulary Words

1. bud
2. but
3. dust
4. fuzz
5. gum
6. hug
7. Judd
8. jump
9. just
10. must
11. Mutt
12. pup
13. rub-a-dub-dub
14. rubs
15. rug
16. snug
17. stuck
18. tub
19. tug
20. umbrella
21. up
22. us

Story Words

23. fill
24. kick
25. swim
26. yell

Gus has a pal.
His pal is Judd.
Gus and Judd have fun in
a cup.

Gus and Judd can swim
in the cup.
Judd can jump up and in.

Gus has an umbrella.
Will Gus get wet?
Yes. Gus will get wet!

Gus can sit on a big bud.
Gus has fun up on the
bud.

Gus fell and got stuck
in gum!
Gus must tug!
Gus must yell to get help.

Judd will help Gus tug.
Puff! Puff!
Gus is not stuck in the
gum.

Gus and Judd run fast
to the hut and stop.
Gus and Judd kick
up dust.

Gus and Judd sit on a rug to rest.
The rug has fuzz.

Mom said, "Is Dad
in the hut?"
"Not yet," said Gus. "It is
just us, Gus and Judd."

Mom will hug a bug, but
Gus has mud and dust.
Mom will not have mud
on the rug.

Dad will fill the tub.
Dad has cut steps in it.
Gus can get up in the
tub.

Rub-a-dub-dub!

Dad rubs a bug in a tub.

Gus must get to bed.
Gus will get Mutt.
Mutt is a pup.

Gus is in bed.
Mutt is in bed.

Gus is snug in his bed.
The End